Oh, Behave!

Manners at the Table

Siân Smith

D0809834

9112000216907

www.raintreepublishers.co.uk
Visit our website to find out more information about Raintree books.

To order:
☎ Phone 0845 6044371
🖷 Fax +44 (0) 1865 312263
📧 Email myorders@raintreepublishers.co.uk

Customers from outside the UK please telephone +44 1865 312262

Raintree is an imprint of Capstone Global Library Limited, a company incorporated in England and Wales having its registered office at 7 Pilgrim Street, London, EC4V 6LB – Registered company number: 6695582

Edited by Dan Nunn, Rebecca Rissman, and John-Paul Wilkins
Designed by Marcus Bell
Picture research by Elizabeth Alexander
Production by Alison Parsons
Originated by Capstone Global Library Ltd
Printed and bound in China by Leo Paper Products Ltd

ISBN 978 1 406 23822 8 (hardback)
16 15 14 13 12
10 9 8 7 6 5 4 3 2 1

ISBN 978 1 406 23827 3 (paperback)
17 16 15 14 13
10 9 8 7 6 5 4 3 2 1

British Library Cataloguing in Publication Data
Smith, Siân.
Manners at the table. -- (Oh, behave!)
395.5'4-dc22
A full catalogue record for this book is available from the British Library.

Acknowledgements
We would like to thank the following for permission to reproduce photographs: © Capstone Publishers pp. 6, 14, 18, 19, 22 (Karon Dubke); Alamy p. 7 (© Tetra Images); Getty Images pp. 9 (Jessie Jean/Taxi), 10 (Sean Locke/Photodisc), 12 (Jose Luis Pelaez Inc/ Blend Images), 13 (Christopher Robbins/Riser), 15, 22 (OJO Images/Robert Daly/Workbook Stock), 17, 22 (fStop Images); iStockphoto pp. 16 (© kate_sept2004), 20, 23 (© Christine Glade); Shutterstock pp. 4, 5 (© Monkey Business Images), 8, 11, 22 (© wavebreakmedia ltd), 21 (© Glenda M. Powers), 23 (© clearviewstock).

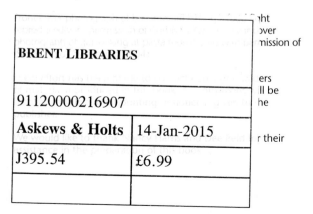

Contents

Good manners

People with good manners know how to behave in different places.

If you have good manners, people will want to eat with you.

Before you eat

Wash your hands before you eat.

Hands that are not clean can
spread germs.

At the table

Wait until everyone has their food before you start eating.

Don't start eating straight away.

Say "please" and "thank you" when you ask for food.

If you do not ask nicely, people will
not want to help you.

Share food with other people.

Don't take more food than you need.

fork

knife

Eat your food with a knife and fork.

Don't eat with your hands unless you have been told that you can.

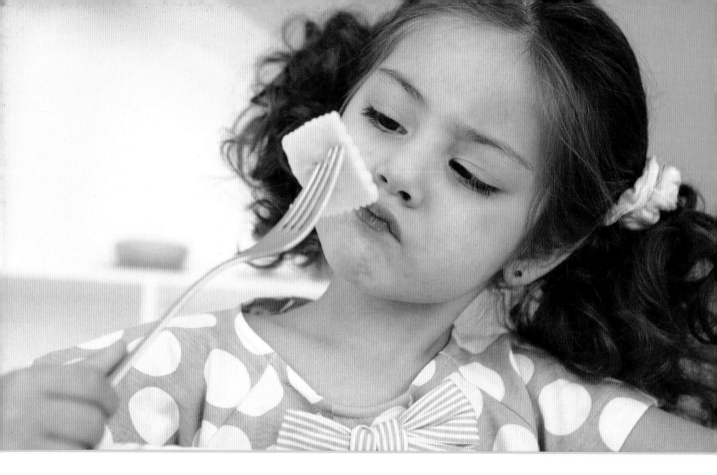

Try to eat some food, even if you think you won't like it.

Don't pull faces. It can hurt people's feelings.

Don't talk when your mouth is full.

Ask if you can leave the table when you have finished.

Wherever you go

Table manners are important at a restaurant.

Table manners are important wherever you eat a meal.

Best behaviour

Which person here has good table manners?

Answer on page 24

Picture glossary

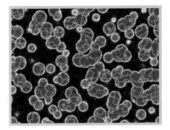

germs tiny living things that can make you ill

good manners ways of behaving politely and well

Index

Answer to question on page 22
The girl asking to leave the table has good manners.

Notes for parents and teachers

Before reading

Explain that good manners are ways of behaving – they help us to understand what to do and how to act. They are important because they show us how to treat each other and help us to get on well with other people. What examples of good manners can the children think of? List these together.

After reading

- Set up a role-play area with a table, chairs, cutlery, plates, cups, and if possible real food and drink. Choose a group of children who think they can demonstrate good table manners. Give them a scenario and characters, for example a child eating at a friend's house. Discuss the good manners being shown together or ask another child to be a "good manners spotter" who can point out examples of good manners being used.

- List the table manners shown in the book together. Can the children think of any more examples to add to the list? Ask them to imagine a child going to eat at a restaurant or at a friend's house for the first time and not knowing how to behave. Help the children to design posters that explain what to do and what not to do.